UNDERSTANDING THE
BLACK LIVES MATTER MOVEMENT

BEING BLACK
IN AMERICA

by Sue Bradford Edwards

BrightP◆int Press

San Diego, CA

BrightPoint Press

© 2021 BrightPoint Press
an imprint of ReferencePoint Press, Inc.
Printed in the United States

For more information, contact:
BrightPoint Press
PO Box 27779
San Diego, CA 92198
www.BrightPointPress.com

LIBRARY OF CONGRESS CATALOGING-IN-PUBLICATION DATA

Names: Edwards, Sue Bradford, author.
Title: Being black in America / by Sue Bradford Edwards.
Description: San Diego, CA : BrightPoint Press, an imprint of ReferencePoint Press, [2021]
  | Series: Understanding the Black Lives Matter movement | Includes bibliographical
  references and index. |
Audience: Grades 7-9 | Summary: "Black Americans face racism and its effects on a daily
  basis. Inequality is present in education, health care, policing, and many other areas of
  life. Being Black in America examines these disparities and looks at proposed solutions to
  make American society more equal."-- Provided by publisher.
Identifiers: LCCN 2020048942 (print) | LCCN 2020048943 (eBook) | ISBN 9781678200688
  (hardcover) | ISBN 9781678200695 (eBook)
Subjects: LCSH: African Americans--Social conditions--21st century--Juvenile literature. |
  African Americans--Civil rights--Juvenile literature. | Race discrimination--United States--
  Juvenile literature. | Anti-racism--United States--Juvenile literature.
Classification: LCC E185.86 .E289 2021 (print) | LCC E185.86 (eBook) | DDC 305.896/073
  --dc23
LC record available at https://lccn.loc.gov/2020048942
LC eBook record available at https://lccn.loc.gov/2020048943

CONTENTS

AT A GLANCE

- Many Black Americans encounter racism in daily life. Racism is discrimination based on race.

- Racism affects getting a job and the type of job a person can get. This can affect the amount of money a person earns. It can control where a person lives. It affects physical and mental health too. It also affects the role the criminal justice system may play in a person's life.

- In 2018, the average white household income was $84,600. The average Black household income was $51,600.

- People in the education, health care, and justice systems may have bias against Black Americans. This can lead to poorer outcomes for Black people.

- In the 2015–2016 school year, 15 percent of public school students were Black. Yet Black students made up 31 percent of all in-school arrests.

- In 2019, 5.4 percent of white Americans had no health insurance. Among Black Americans, the number was 9.7 percent.

- In 2016, Black youth made up 15 percent of the children in the United States. They made up 35 percent of the young people arrested.

- On May 25, 2020, George Floyd died in police custody. Protests associated with the Black Lives Matter movement, which seeks to end violence and discrimination against Black people, erupted across the United States.

PROTESTING INJUSTICE

George Floyd died on May 25, 2020, in Minneapolis, Minnesota, after a police officer knelt on his neck for several minutes. A week later, the area where he died had been turned into a memorial. People had painted a large mural of Floyd.

Nineteen-year-old Izaiah Yeager arrived. He was with his two brothers and his dad,

People created a memorial with flowers, signs, and artwork near the spot where Floyd had died.

Corey Yeager. Corey was a psychologist

for the Detroit Pistons basketball team.

Also with them were Shawn Shipman and

his two sons. Shipman worked for the

public school system. The young men knelt. Each thrust a fist into the air. They bowed their heads.

"Our situation is grave. If you are Black, born in America, you have and will experience trauma. This is a country where a Black man can be murdered for jogging, a Black woman can be murdered while sleeping, and then there is George Floyd and the many, many George Floyds," Corey said to a reporter.[1]

Izaiah also spoke to a reporter. He shared rules his father gave him. Be alert. Know who is watching you. If you see

Many Black families have discussions about racism with their children.

police while driving, slow down. Many Black

parents share rules like these to keep their

children safe. They know the extra risks that

Black people face in America.

FLOYD'S DEATH SPARKS PROTESTS

Floyd had bought cigarettes at a grocery

store. The clerk called 911 to report that

Floyd had used fake money. The police arrived. They handcuffed Floyd. He resisted when the officers tried to put him in the police car. Floyd said he was afraid of enclosed spaces.

Floyd fell to the ground, and Officer Derek Chauvin knelt on his neck. Floyd said he could not breathe. He stopped moving after almost eight minutes. At the hospital, medical staff declared Floyd dead.

After Floyd died, protests took place across the United States. People spoke against racial injustice. They talked about **discrimination** in its many forms. They

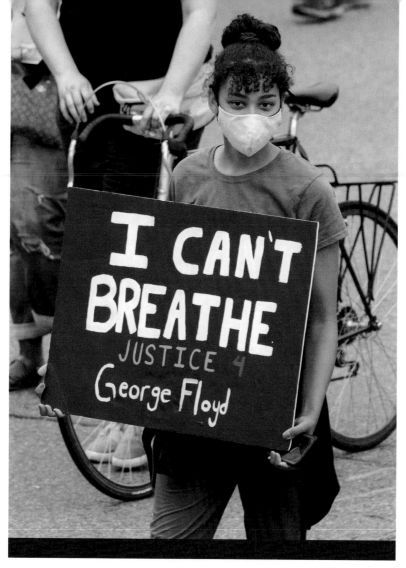

Floyd's death inspired a wave of protests and activism against racism throughout the country.

demanded equality in education and

employment. Black Americans and their

supporters were tired of everyday racism.

CHAPTER ONE

HOW DO BLACK STUDENTS EXPERIENCE RACISM?

Racism is discrimination against people based on their race. Race is not based on biology. It is a socially created idea. There is overlap between the ideas of race and ethnicity. Discrimination based on these two things is often linked.

Race does not have a basis in biology. It is an idea that society has developed to divide people into groups.

People who believe racist ideas may think people of one race are better than others. They may think things like honesty or sports skills are based on race. In the United States, Black people are common targets of racism. Many experience racism in schools.

Some people hold racist beliefs and act in racist ways intentionally. But others may not see how racist ideas affect how they act. This is known as implicit **bias**. For example, it can happen when a teacher watches preschool students play. A chatty white student may be seen as eager. The teacher might think this student loves school. A chatty Black student may be seen as badly behaved. The teacher might think this student is too loud.

These judgments can set students down different paths. The eager student is praised and gets awards. He is placed in gifted

Bias can begin to affect students even at a very young age.

classes. When he gets old enough, school staff helps him find money for college. A badly behaved student is scolded and gets sent to the office more often. She is suspended. In high school, the staff does not talk to her about college.

In this way, race can affect a person's success in school. Internalized racism makes the problem worse. This happens when people absorb racist ideas about themselves. A Black student is told she is bad. Teachers say she is loud and does not behave. The student may start to believe the things she is told. She does not sign up for the hardest classes. She does not ask about college.

MICROAGGRESSIONS

Microaggressions are comments and actions that show bias. They may not be intentional. But they still harm the victim.

Microaggressions may seem small, but they can be deeply hurtful for those affected.

Sometimes they are against LGBTQ people.

They may be directed at women. Often they

are related to a person's race.

Racist microaggressions affect Black

students. Microaggressions may be jokes or

even compliments. They hold hidden racist assumptions. A Black student who speaks a certain way may be told he sounds white. This may imply that Black people misuse English. A Black student may be asked if she plays basketball. The assumption is that Black people must all play sports. A student may be told she is lucky to be Black because this will help her get into college. This implies that she will not have earned her place.

In other microaggressions, Black students are ignored in class. The teacher only calls on white students. Yet when there

is trouble, the Black students are the first ones questioned.

Micro means small. To an outsider, microaggressions can seem small. But their impact is big. Microaggressions at school cause stress for students. They undermine faith that students have in themselves.

ELIMINATING MICROAGGRESSIONS

Psychologist Derald W. Sue shared ways to avoid carrying out microaggressions. He says people can be aware of personal biases. They can seek out people who are unlike themselves. If someone says something is a microaggression, people should not become defensive. They should listen. They should consider what was said and how it made people feel.

The students may become angry. They start to dislike school. Microaggressions can even lead to depression. Students may develop ways to cope with repeated microaggressions. But the impact can still be severe.

INSTITUTIONAL RACISM

Institutional racism is how power works in a society to harm people based on race. It is about who has power and who does not. Rules and laws are part of it. So are the people who apply them.

Institutional racism affects Black students. It occurs when schools work

Racism can affect the experiences of Black students in a wide variety of ways.

against Black students. Schools with mostly

Black students may lack resources that

white schools have. And schools may make

Black people feel targeted or unwelcome.

This happens in several ways.

Teachers and principals are the faces

of their schools. When Black students

see teachers who look like themselves, they may feel safer. They may trust Black teachers to be fairer. When students feel safe, they work harder. They get better test scores. They are more likely to think education is important.

In 2017, American University published a study. Low-income Black male students in third, fourth, and fifth grade with one Black teacher were 39 percent likelier to stay in school compared to those with no Black teachers. In 2019, the National Bureau of Economic Research did a similar study. Its report found that having a Black teacher

EDUCATION AND RACE

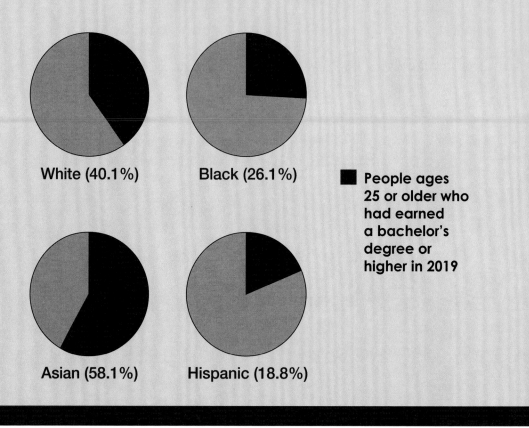

White (40.1%)   Black (26.1%)

■ People ages 25 or older who had earned a bachelor's degree or higher in 2019

Asian (58.1%)   Hispanic (18.8%)

"US Census Bureau Releases New Educational Attainment Data," US Census Bureau, March 30, 2020. www.census.gov.

in elementary school made Black students 13 percent more likely to go to college.

In America, teachers often do not reflect the Black student body. In 2019,

the *Washington Post* surveyed school districts. It found that only 7 percent of Black students went to schools with a significant number of Black teachers. Those districts were defined as having at least as large a percentage of Black teachers as Black students.

Activists are pushing for equality in school resources. And more Black teachers are being trained. But it will take time before they are in the classroom. "For the foreseeable future, Black kids are going to go to school and face white female teachers," said Nicholas Papageorge.

Having teachers who look like them and who may share their experiences can make a difference for Black students.

Papageorge is a professor at Johns Hopkins University. "We also need to educate white teachers about implicit bias," said Papageorge.[2] Implicit bias is unconscious. People do not know they have it. Yet it affects how they act.

SCHOOL DISCIPLINE

Institutional racism also affects school discipline. Schools with zero-tolerance policies suspend or expel students who get in fights. In theory, any student who fights will be suspended. But school staff decides who actually gets punished.

On average, Black students are three times likelier to get suspended than white students. They are almost four times as likely to get expelled. Suspended and expelled students may drop out of school. Those who drop out are three times more likely to get arrested.

In the 2015–2016 school year, Black students made up 15 percent of public school students. Yet they were 31 percent of the students arrested at school. These students enter the criminal justice system. This trend has become known as the school-to-prison pipeline.

RESTORATIVE JUSTICE

Detention and suspension are not the only ways to handle behavior issues at school. Some schools use restorative justice. It does not focus on punishment. When students argue with other students or teachers, they sit down to talk. With the help of a **mediator**, they discuss the issue instead of fighting. They come to a resolution. The student at fault might do service, such as helping clean the cafeteria.

CHAPTER TWO

HOW DOES RACISM IMPACT WHERE PEOPLE LIVE?

B eing Black impacts how much money a person can make. The Pew Research Center reports on income levels in the United States. The white median household income in 2018 was $84,600. This meant half of all white households

Racism can affect the kinds of places where people live in many ways.

made more. Half made less. The Black

median household income for 2018 was

only $51,600.

Inequality can be seen in poverty

figures too. The poverty rate among

white Americans in 2019 was 7.3 percent. The rate among Black Americans was 18.8 percent.

DISCRIMINATION IN EMPLOYMENT

Black workers often do different jobs than white workers. In April 2020 the COVID-19 **pandemic** was happening. Many businesses closed. But some workers were considered essential. The Economic Policy Institute found that one in nine workers overall was Black. One in six essential workers was Black. These people work in grocery and drug stores. They work in public transit. They have jobs as truckers

and in warehouses. They work for the post office. They have jobs in health care and in child care. These jobs often pay less than office jobs. People in these jobs were at a higher risk of getting COVID-19.

A college degree can help a person get a higher-paying job. But Black graduates still face challenges. A study compared what happens when Black workers and white

COVID UNEMPLOYMENT

During the COVID-19 pandemic, unemployment in the United States rose. For white workers, the rate rose from 3.1 percent in February 2020 to 14.2 percent in April. For Black workers, the rate rose from 5.8 percent to 16.7 percent in that time.

workers seek jobs. The workers in the study were equally qualified. White job hunters got 36 percent more callbacks than Black **applicants**. A callback is when someone is asked to come in for an interview. These people are more likely to get a job.

Racism does not end when a Black worker gets a job. "It's one more area where we have to put on the mask to fit in. We get trained in how to do that from an early age," says Monica Williams.[3] Williams is a Black clinical psychologist at the University of Ottawa. Fitting in may mean acting extra cheerful. Some people try to never

Racism in the workplace can be a hurdle to earning a higher income.

disagree. Bosses and coworkers might be

influenced by negative stereotypes about

Black workers. They might judge those

employees more harshly. Racism impacts

the jobs Black workers get. It also means

they have less money to spend on housing

than white workers.

HOUSING DISCRIMINATION

Redlining is a type of institutional racism. It started in the 1930s. Banks refused to help people buy homes in certain neighborhoods.

Houses cost a lot of money. When people buy houses, they borrow money from the bank. This money is called a loan.

In redlining, someone would ask to borrow money to buy a house. Bank staff would look at a map. If the neighborhood was outlined in red, or redlined, the bank would say no. These redlined neighborhoods were considered high

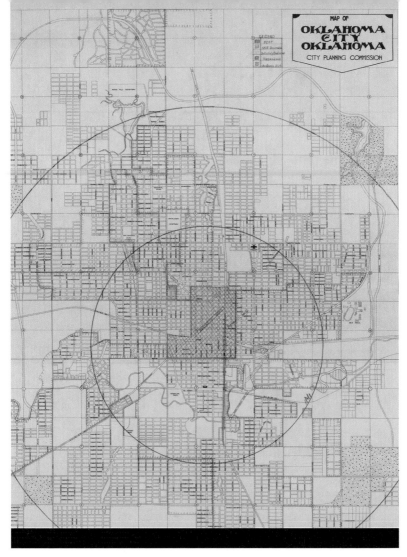

This map of Oklahoma City from the 1930s shows red lines around certain neighborhoods.

risk. The bankers believed people in these

neighborhoods would not repay the loans.

The people in these neighborhoods were

mostly Black or Hispanic. This made it difficult for these people to own homes.

A Black person might want to buy a home in a white neighborhood. But many neighborhoods had restrictive rules in the mid-1900s called racial covenants. People of color were barred from buying homes in these areas. Many Black people could only rent apartments and homes. They often lived in the cities. White homeowners lived in the suburbs. Redlining and racial covenants led to **segregated** housing.

Segregation also affects where jobs are available. Many Black workers have

Traveling a long way to work can be difficult if a person doesn't have access to quick transportation.

service jobs. These jobs may not be near where they live. Employees have to travel far from home to get to work. This can be challenging if they lack good transportation.

The US government made redlining and racial covenants illegal in 1968.

Yet segregation and the damage it causes continue. Living in segregated areas can rob people of opportunities. Being unable to buy homes prevents people from building up wealth over generations.

SUCCESS DOES NOT STOP RACIAL PROFILING

Racism impacts the kinds of jobs Black people get. This affects how much money they make and where they can live. But even those who live in wealthy neighborhoods suffer from racism. They are still the victims of racial profiling.

Racial profiling is a racist police practice. In profiling, race is used to determine if someone might be a criminal. Profiling is one way police decide which drivers to pull over.

Profiling affects many Black people, including those in positions of

TRAFFIC STOPS

Police make more than 50,000 traffic stops in the United States each day. They pull over cars. They question drivers. Stanford University gathers information on these stops. It publishes this data in its Open Policing Project. Stanford found that Black drivers are more likely than white drivers to be stopped and ticketed. They are more likely to have their cars searched.

Representative Danny K. Davis is among the Black politicians who have spoken about personal experiences with racial profiling.

power. Danny K. Davis is a Black US

Representative from Illinois. Police pulled

him over in Chicago. They accused him of

driving over the center line, but Davis said

he did not. He believed the stop was racially

motivated. He said, "I had to conclude that race had to have entered the picture, and that the only reason we were stopped is that there were four African-Americans . . . in a car going down the street."[4]

Police are more likely to find a Black person in a wealthy neighborhood suspicious. Todd Cox is a director at the Center for American Progress. He went to the University of Pennsylvania, which is in a wealthy area. He is Black. He recalled being stopped by police when walking home from school. Cox knew he had done nothing wrong. His parents had taught him how to

act with the police. But being stopped was still scary.

Another major case of racial profiling happened in 2009. Black Harvard professor Henry Louis Gates Jr. was at his Massachusetts home. But his front door was jammed, and he couldn't get in. His taxi driver helped him force open the door. Someone in the neighborhood called the police, and an officer arrived. Gates felt he was being profiled. He became frustrated and angry as he spoke with the officer. The officer arrested him. Gates was released hours later. But the incident made

The 2009 arrest of Henry Louis Gates Jr. brought national attention to the issue of racial profiling.

national headlines. People noted that even a successful professor could not avoid being profiled.

CHAPTER THREE

HOW DOES RACISM AFFECT HEALTH?

Black Americans face poorer health outcomes than their white counterparts. Black patients are diagnosed with higher rates of diabetes, obesity, and **asthma**. In 2017, 12.6 percent of Black children had asthma. Only 7.7 percent of white children had asthma.

Some health issues, including asthma, are more common in Black children than in white children.

One factor affecting the health of Black Americans is environmental injustice. Black neighborhoods are more likely to be in areas with pollution. Homes may be near factories, power plants, or highways.

Pollution in these places can make health problems such as asthma worse.

Having one illness can make another more serious. Consider asthma, diabetes, hypertension, or obesity. People with these diseases face more danger from COVID-19. This is one reason that a disproportionate number of Black patients die from COVID-19. Black people may also be more exposed to COVID-19 due to their jobs, making the problem worse.

"In Michigan, over 40 percent of COVID-19 deaths are African Americans, while only 14 percent of the population

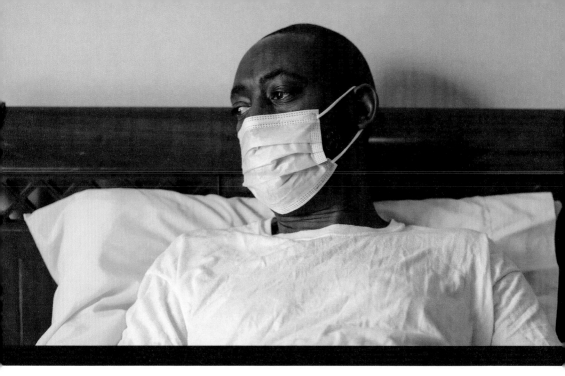

Black patients face a higher risk from COVID-19 on average than their white counterparts.

is made up of African Americans. This is

significant," said Dr. David J. Brown.[5] Brown

works at the University of Michigan Medical

School. He is an associate vice president

and associate dean.

The Black community also faces other

health problems. Black Americans suffer

Black mothers and babies face greater risks during childbirth than those of other races.

higher infant and maternal mortality than other groups. This means that more newborn babies and mothers die. Black Americans also have the highest cancer death rates of any group.

"It's the fact that we see an undeniable burden of disease in the black population,"

said Dr. Melissa Creary.[6] Creary is a professor of public health. She works at the University of Michigan. Health care professionals are learning why Black Americans are more likely to get sick. Stress is one cause. Lack of access to health care and healthy food are other causes. Racism plays a part in each.

HOW RACISM LIMITS HEALTH CARE

A big part of staying well is access to health care. Health insurance helps people pay for health care. When people get sick, they visit a doctor. They get medicine. They go to the hospital. They might have physical

therapy. Physical therapy is exercise that helps a person get well. All of this is expensive. Health insurance can help pay for these bills. But people have to pay for health insurance.

President Barack Obama signed the Affordable Care Act (ACA). It became law in March 2010. This act gave more people access to health insurance. Under the act, 20 million people gained health insurance. This included 2.8 million Black Americans. Still, Black Americans are more likely to be uninsured than white Americans. In 2019, 9.7 percent of Black Americans

The signing of the Affordable Care Act extended health insurance to many more people, but millions more still lacked insurance coverage.

were uninsured. Only 5.4 percent of white Americans lacked insurance.

Health insurance helps pay part of a person's health care bills. But even with insurance, the costs can be devastating. The average family spends $8,200 each year on health care. That is 11 percent of

the average family's income. The average

Black family makes less. That $8,200 per

year in health costs would be 20 percent

of the average Black family's income. Many

Black patients cannot afford the health care

they need.

Segregation also affects health care.

Mostly Black communities have fewer

BENEFIT FROM BLACK DOCTORS

Studies show that Black doctors benefit Black patients. Black doctors are less likely to have bias against Black people. They are more likely to understand how Black patients live. Black patients are more likely to do what Black doctors say. They also work better with Black doctors to make health care choices.

doctors. There are also fewer hospitals. When Black patients do see a professional, they often get lower quality health care. Bias from doctors or nurses can affect the care the patients receive. For example, studies show that health care workers commonly underestimate the severity of pain in Black patients. This can be a case of implicit bias.

Black women face additional challenges. They are much more likely than white women to die when giving birth. The difference continues even when researchers consider factors like education and income. Racism toward Black women

can significantly affect their health

care outcomes.

FOOD INSECURITY

Racism also impacts health through food

insecurity. When people do not have access

to healthful food, they have food insecurity.

They may not get enough to eat. Or what

they can buy may not be nutritious.

Many Black people live in neighborhoods

without large grocery stores. Instead,

people shop at convenience stores. A lot of

the food in convenience stores is packaged.

Packaged foods include snack cakes,

chips, and candy. These stores may also

Unhealthful snack food is often easier to find in neighborhood convenience stores than more nutritious options.

sell foods such as hot dogs or pizza. These things are cheap. But they are high in sugar and fat. They are not healthful. It may be harder to find fresh fruits and vegetables in these neighborhoods. Such neighborhoods are often called food deserts.

A group called Feeding America collected information on food insecurity. It identified the ten counties with the highest rates of food insecurity. At least 60 percent of the people living in these counties were Black. Food insecurity damages the health of many Black Americans.

HUNGER AND HEALTH

Food insecurity can lead to hunger, which has health consequences. One in four Black children does not get enough to eat. If a pregnant woman is hungry, she may give birth to an underweight baby. These babies get sick more often. Hunger is also linked to diabetes and cancer.

STRESS

Racism affects health by causing stress too. Stress wears down the human body. This makes it harder to fight off illness. Research shows that stress, such as stress caused by racism, can lead to heart attacks. Stress also contributes to cancer and nerve diseases.

Racism impacts the health of Black Americans. It can lead to disease. It can make it harder for them to see a doctor. It can make them distrust the health care system. And it can make it harder for them to get well.

CHAPTER FOUR

HOW DOES RACISM AFFECT JUSTICE?

The United States has the world's largest criminal justice system. In 2020, about 2.3 million people were incarcerated. The United States has a larger percentage of its population in prison than any other country. Not all Americans are at equal risk. According to 2016 data, Black adults are

A long history of inequality in the justice system has harmed the Black community.

5.9 times more likely than white adults to be imprisoned.

One factor in this difference came from President Richard Nixon. Nixon declared a War on Drugs in 1971. "America's public

enemy number one . . . is drug abuse,"

he said.[7] He targeted illegal drug use and

sales. Users and dealers were arrested. If

people were convicted of a drug crime, they

went to jail for a set time. Nixon created the

Drug Enforcement Agency (DEA) in 1973.

Today, the DEA has 5,000 agents. Their job

is to stop drug use and drug smuggling.

In 1994, *Harper's Magazine* interviewed

John Ehrlichman. Ehrlichman had been in

charge of Nixon's domestic policies. He

spoke with reporter Dan Baum. He said

Nixon considered Black people his political

enemies. He wanted to be reelected for a

President Nixon's War on Drugs policies often targeted Black people.

second presidential term. Nixon thought

Black voters would choose his opponent.

The War on Drugs targeted them. It

disrupted the Black community.

Drug enforcement continues to target

Black people. Black and white Americans

use some drugs at nearly the same rates.

But Black Americans are arrested more

for violations with those types of drugs.

The American Civil Liberties Union (ACLU)

studied arrest records. Black marijuana

users were 3.7 times more likely to be

arrested than white users.

STOP-AND-FRISK

Black Americans are often the victims of

stop-and-frisk. In stop-and-frisk, an officer

stops someone on the street. The officer

pats this person down. He or she is looking

for a weapon.

Protesters have spoken out about stop-and-frisk policies.

Stop-and-frisk has a long history. It became widely used in New York City. It peaked there in 2011. That year, New York City police stopped almost 700,000 people. Police are supposed to stop someone only if they think the person committed a crime. Simply being a certain race or ethnicity does not justify being stopped. Yet 84 percent of those stopped in 2011 were Black or Hispanic people.

PRETRIAL DETENTION AND SENTENCING

In 2016, Black youth made up 15 percent of US children. But they were 35 percent of the young people arrested. Black

Americans are also held in local jails more often. This happens 3.5 times as often as it does to white Americans. They are often being held pretrial. This means they are held until their trial. Pretrial prisoners make up 65 percent of the US jail population.

FAIR SENTENCING ACT

Cocaine is an illegal drug, and crack is one form of cocaine. Studies show that white people use cocaine at a higher rate than other groups. Black people use crack at a higher rate than other groups. For many years the legal penalties for crack were much harsher than for cocaine. This affected Black people who were charged. The US Congress passed the Fair **Sentencing** Act in 2010. This law reduced the difference between penalties for crack and cocaine.

Inequalities in the justice system have led to large numbers of Black Americans in prisons.

In 70 percent of all pretrial releases, people had to pay bail. Bail is cash paid before a person is released. If the person does not return for trial, they lose the money. Black prisoners are more likely to be refused bail. If bail is set, their bail is more likely to be higher than they can pay. They must wait in jail until their trials.

There are also racial inequalities in sentencing. Black Americans get sentenced to prison more often. They also get longer sentences. Laws sometimes force courts to give minimum sentences for certain crimes. Black defendants are twice as likely to get

charged with those crimes compared to white defendants in similar situations.

Black men are particularly affected by these inequalities. Their imprisonment rates rise very high in some states. In eleven states, at least 5 percent of Black men are in prison. The rate is highest in Oklahoma. There, about 6.7 percent of Black men are in prison.

LIFE AFTER PRISON

Once people are released from prison, they have to start a new life. This means that they have to find a job. They have to find a home. They have to feed themselves.

In 2010, about 8 percent of American adults had a felony conviction. The rate among Black adults was 23 percent. Many had served their time. But they had still lost access to some government aid.

PAROLE

Parole is the release of a prisoner before serving his or her full sentence. The person must have a good in-prison record and show good behavior. The *New York Times* investigated parole practices. It found that the conduct of Black prisoners is judged more harshly. They get parole less often. In addition, paroled people can be returned to prison. This happens most often to Black parolees.

In 1996, the Welfare Reform Act became law. It said that people with drug convictions could not get certain kinds of aid. This includes food stamps. Most states later backed off. By 2020, only a few of them still fully enforced a lifetime ban on food stamps.

Assistance can be vital. Employers might not hire someone who has been convicted of a crime. Researchers found that white job applicants with criminal records were more likely to receive positive responses from potential employers than were Black applicants with no records. Black applicants

Activists in many states have pushed for people with felony records to have their voting rights restored.

with records may have a hard time getting

interviews at all.

In many states, a person with a felony

record cannot vote. In some states this

ban is for life. Because of disparities in

Activists are pushing for an end to racism and discrimination in all their forms.

sentencing, this affects Black Americans at a high rate. These people have served their sentences. Yet they have no voice in American government. They cannot vote for change.

Being Black in America does not need to be a hardship. Black teachers can be hired. Black doctors can be trained. People can work to eliminate institutional racism. They can learn to avoid bias and microaggressions. Police practices that have racist effects can be reformed. Change can happen.

GLOSSARY

applicants

people applying for a job

asthma

a disease that causes trouble with breathing

bias

an unfair prejudice against people from a certain group

discrimination

treating people differently because they belong to a certain group

mediator

a person who helps two people in conflict come to a resolution

pandemic

an outbreak of disease that occurs over a wide area

segregated

separated based on a trait such as race

sentencing

the process of determining what punishment a person faces for a crime

SOURCE NOTES

INTRODUCTION: PROTESTING INJUSTICE

1. Quoted in Janell Ross, "The Toll of Everyday Racism on Black Americans," *NBC News*, June 3, 2020. www.nbcnews.com.

CHAPTER ONE: HOW DO BLACK STUDENTS EXPERIENCE RACISM?

2. Quoted in Lauren Camera, "Black Teachers Improve Outcomes for Black Students," *US News and World Report*, November 23, 2018. www.usnews.com.

CHAPTER TWO: HOW DOES RACISM IMPACT WHERE PEOPLE LIVE?

3. Quoted in Ben Jay, "White Job Applicants Are 2.5 Times More Likely to Get Hired, Northwestern Study Finds," *Acorns*, June 17, 2020. https://grow.acorns.com.

4. Quoted in Catrin Einhorn, "Congressman Sees Bias in Chicago Traffic Stop," *New York Times*, November 24, 2007. www.nytimes.com.

CHAPTER THREE: HOW DOES RACISM AFFECT HEALTH?

5. Quoted in Jina Sawani and Kelly Malcom, "Racial Disparities in the Time of COVID-19," *University of Michigan Health Lab*, May 4, 2020. https://labblog.uofmhealth.org.

6. Quoted in Sawani and Malcom, "Racial Disparities in the Time of COVID-19."

CHAPTER FOUR: HOW DOES RACISM AFFECT JUSTICE?

7. Quoted in "President Nixon Declares Drug Abuse 'Public Enemy Number One,'" *Richard Nixon Foundation*, April 29, 2016. www.youtube.com.

FOR FURTHER RESEARCH

BOOKS

Wade Hudson and Cheryl Willis Hudson, eds., *The Talk: Conversations About Race, Love and Truth.* New York: Crown Books for Young Readers, 2020.

Tiffany Jewell, *This Book Is Anti-Racist.* London: Frances Lincoln, 2020.

Jason Reynolds and Ibram X. Kendi, *Stamped: Racism, Antiracism, and You.* New York: Little, Brown and Company, 2020.

Rachael L. Thomas, *#BlackLivesMatter: Protesting Racism.* Minneapolis, MN: Abdo, 2020.

INTERNET SOURCES

"Being Black in America: 'We Have a Place in This World Too,'" *NPR*, June 5, 2020. www.npr.org.

"Report to the United Nations on Racial Disparities in the US Criminal Justice System," *The Sentencing Project*, April 19, 2018. www.sentencingproject.org.

"Thirty Years of America's Drug War: A Chronology," *PBS Frontline*, 2014. www.pbs.org.

WEBSITES

National Education Association: Racial and Social Justice
www.nea.org/advocating-for-change/racial-social-justice

This website includes information on how teachers and schools are working against systemic racism and other forms of discrimination.

Robert Wood Johnson Foundation: Racism and Health
www.rwjf.org/en/library/collections/racism-and-health.html

This website collects a variety of information on how racism has negative effects on people's health.

The Urban Institute: Justice Policy Center
https://urban.org/policy-centers/justice-policy-center

The Justice Policy Center combats racism as part of its mission to improve safety and fight crime. Its website includes information on jails, imprisonment, and improving relations between police and communities.

INDEX

IMAGE CREDITS

ABOUT THE AUTHOR

Sue Bradford Edwards is a Missouri nonfiction author. She writes about social science, history, and science. The author of 29 books for children, her books include *Hidden Human Computers*, *Black Lives Matter*, and *What Are Race and Racism?*